HOW TO
FLOURISH IN LIFE

PRINCIPLES FOR BUILDING A THRIVING, PRODUCTIVE LIFE

HOW TO FLOURISH IN LIFE

PRINCIPLES FOR BUILDING A THRIVING, PRODUCTIVE LIFE

BRIAN HOUSTON

PUBLISHED BY MAXIMISED LEADERSHIP

How to flourish in life
First published July 2003
Second printing November 2003

Houston, Brian
ISBN 09 577336 8 2

Back cover photo of Brian Houston by Femia Shirtliff
Photo of Hillsong Church in worship by David Anderson

Printed by J S McMillan Printing Group, South Granville NSW

Published by Maximised Leadership,
PO Box 1195, Castle Hill NSW 1765 Australia

DEDICATION

GOD'S PEOPLE SHOULD FLOURISH

I have two great passions: one is to build the Church of Jesus Christ, and the other is to help God's people fulfil their potential in life. The fact is that both of these are inter-related and each one supports the other. When the Church thrives, God's people are equipped to fulfil their potential, and when God's people flourish, they instinctively build His Church.

One of my favourite scriptures is found in Psalm 92:

'Those who are planted in the House of the Lord shall flourish in the courts of our God. They shall still bear fruit in old age; they shall be fresh and flourishing.' [Psalm 92:13-14]

A revelation of this powerful promise of God can change your life and produce wonderful results across the span of your life. When you decide to plant yourself in God's House, you *will* thrive. Not only can I testify to this in my own life, but that of my family, my ministry colleagues and our church congregation. The fruit is evident for all to see.

We all face challenges and obstacles at various times, but God's will is for you to flourish and succeed in every area of your life – from your relationships to your career, in your health and finances, to your spiritual life and your church.

The Bible is full of promise and encouragement to this end and there is no reason why you should settle for anything less than God's best. The wonderful thing is that He has set you up to flourish in life because He has deposited *seeds of the highest potential* within you. No matter what you are facing right now or where you are positioned, God has so much more in store for you.

I pray this book will give you some great insights into how you can live at the highest level of life purposed for you, because you were created and destined to flourish and go from strength to strength.

'THOSE WHO ARE
PLANTED IN THE
HOUSE OF THE LORD
SHALL FLOURISH IN THE
COURTS OF OUR GOD '

[PSALM 92:13]

There is nothing I like better than to see God's people expanding and increasing in every area of their lives. I believe you are alive to make a difference, and an increased life empowers you to impact and influence others in a positive way.

There are some who would argue against the need for Christians to be prosperous or successful, but I present this question: Is it an *option* for believers to flourish when it is in their hand to do so, or is it a *responsibility*? In fact, there are three important reasons why God's people should live flourishing lives.

Firstly, when we flourish across every aspect of our lives, we are aligning ourselves with the objectives of Jesus. He said:

'I have come that they may have life, and that they may have it more abundantly.' [John 10:10]

God's purpose and intention is clearly that we should have an abundant life – that means bountiful, productive, successful, prosperous … and flourishing! This kind of abundant life reveals and demonstrates the power of God to others.

The second reason why I believe it is important for God's people to flourish is that it empowers us to have a greater impact. Our ability to make a difference in the lives of others is limited if we are crippled by debt, sickness or emotional dysfunction. Certainly, our God is a present help for anyone in trouble, but His purpose is to help people to overcome these difficulties so we can be in a position of strength to help others.

Thirdly, I believe if people cannot flourish, they are unlikely to stay planted. The House of the Lord should be an environment where people can flourish and become who God purposed them to be. I don't believe God intended His Church to remain small and contained, but rather to keep expanding and enlarging, giving people an opportunity to reach their potential.

'THEY SHALL BE
FRESH AND
FLOURISHING'

(LIT. FAT AND GREEN)

[PSALM 92:14]

When I first started teaching on the subject of 'God's People Should Flourish,' I began to examine the way Psalm 92 describes those who are planted in the House of the Lord: '*They shall be fresh and flourishing*.' In the reference margin of my Bible, the note says that fresh means *fat* and flourishing means *green* like a healthy tree.

I had some fun with our congregation at the time, telling them that God's will for them was to be fat and green, and also full of sap (Psalm 104 says, 'The trees of the Lord are full of sap').

I then went on to tell them that my desire was to build a church of 'fat, green saps'. For a number of weeks these became the buzz words in church life. In fact, one young girl had a bright green T-shirt made for herself, emblazoned with the words, 'FAT AND GREEN!'

While the words literally refer to the qualities of a plant, they also give us a clear picture of what our lives should look like: *fat* in terms of our lives being prosperous, expansive and full of Kingdom purpose; *green* in terms of being healthy, growing and producing fruit.

As a Senior Pastor, I have to ask myself a very important question: *Can the people in our church flourish under my ministry? And if not, why would they stay planted?* I believe it is necessary for believers to be in a local church that facilitates growth and expansion in their lives. If not, they would be better off finding a place where they can flourish.

Psalm 92 states, 'Those who are *planted* in the House of the Lord shall flourish in the courts of our God.' It doesn't say, 'Those who *attend* the House of the Lord' but 'those who are *planted* in the House of the Lord.' There is a difference. To be successful and to prosper in the way God intended requires you to be planted. Not everyone who attends church will flourish, but the promise is to those who are planted.

'YET I HAD PLANTED
YOU A NOBLE VINE,
A SEED OF HIGHEST
QUALITY...'

[JEREMIAH 2:21]

SEEDS OF POTENTIAL

It is impossible to plant tomato seeds and reap carrots. Tomato seeds will produce tomatoes; orange seeds will produce oranges. Within each seed is the potential to produce and reproduce a specific kind of fruit.

Have you ever wondered why the Bible uses the term 'the *seed* of Abraham' or 'the *seed* of David'? It does so because the seed of spiritual destiny and potential is carried from generation to generation. Within every living thing is deposited a seed with the ability to reproduce itself. This is how God created it to be. The Bible says:

'Yet I had planted you a noble vine, a seed of highest quality. How then have you turned before Me into the degenerate plant of an alien vine?' [Jeremiah 2:21]

These words describe how He has deposited within each of us seeds of the highest quality and calibre, which are purposed to grow into a 'noble vine'. These are the seeds of great potential which enable us to succeed and thrive in every area of life, including business, ministry, relationships and health.

Yet in spite of the reality that these seeds of excellence and distinction are planted within everyone, so many people can tragically become degenerate or inferior versions of what God intends them to be. An 'alien vine' is how the scripture describes it.

So what does it take for a seed of the highest quality to become the fat, green noble vine that God intends it to be? There are three basic requirements for a plant to thrive. Firstly, it needs to be planted in *good soil*; secondly, it needs to be *watered or nourished regularly*; and thirdly, the *environment* surrounding it determines how well it will flourish.

Psalm 92 gives a wonderful analogy of a seed planted in fertile soil. It thrives and bears fruit – this is what our lives should look like too.

'... HOW THEN HAVE
YOU TURNED BEFORE
ME INTO
THE DEGENERATE PLANT
OF AN ALIEN VINE?

[JEREMIAH 2:21]

S o if God has placed seeds of the highest quality within us, why is it that so many lives fall short of His finest? How is it possible for a seed of the highest quality to become an alien vine? This verse in Jeremiah reveals the reason:

'Your own wickedness will correct you, and your backslidings will rebuke you. Know therefore and see that it is an evil and bitter thing that you have forsaken the Lord your God.' [Jeremiah 2:19]

Israel was destined to inherit God's blessing and promise, but they began to backslide from God. To backslide literally means to lose all forward momentum. The moment you stop moving forward in Christ is the moment you stop growing, and other things (alien to God's heart for you) begin to flourish instead of His purposes.

In some churches, for example, a vine of negativity, disunity and even carnality flourishes, instead of a vine of encouragement, unity and true spirituality.

You may know people who were once actively involved in their local church but gradually began to fall away from serving God. The seeds of the highest quality which began to flourish became withered and stunted. Instead of emerging into a noble vine, they became an 'alien vine' – alien to the purposes of God.

The Bible describes such people in this way:

'They are like stunted shrubs in the desert, with no hope for the future.' [Jeremiah 17:6 NLT]

This paints a bleak picture of someone who was once growing but now stands paralysed in a dry desert wasteland–purposeless and hopeless. Within them a seed of the highest quality still remains, and often all it takes is some good fertile soil and regular nourishment to revive it. Remember, where there is life, there is hope!

'BEHOLD, IT IS PLANTED,
WILL IT THRIVE?
WILL IT NOT UTTERLY
WITHER WHEN THE EAST
WIND TOUCHES IT?'

[EZEKIEL 17:10]

I am committed to building a healthy church where people are nourished so they can flourish and grow as God intended.

As already stated, the promise of a flourishing life is not for those who *attend* church but those who are *planted* in His House. Being planted means you allow your roots to go deep.

When you buy a particular tree or shrub from a nursery, it usually comes with a label describing the ideal conditions for it to flourish. Some do better in full sun, and others in shady, damp conditions. The key is to plant it correctly. The fact is that many people are also planted incorrectly and the fruit of their lives proves the reality of this point.

The Bible asks this question:

'Behold, it is planted, will it thrive? Will it not utterly wither when the east wind touches it? It will wither in the garden terrace where it grew.' [Ezekiel 17:10]

You may be planted but can you thrive? If you are planted exactly where God has purposed you to be, the conditions should be favourable for successful growth.

Psalm 1 is a great illustration of a flourishing life and carries a promise for those planted in a life-giving location.

'He shall be like a tree planted by the rivers of water, that brings forth its fruit in its season, whose leaf also shall not wither; and whatever he does shall prosper.' [Psalm 1:3]

When you are planted in the right place and in an environment designed to shape your 'seeds of the highest quality', you will produce fruit in the right or perfect season, you will grow stronger and taller, and you will flourish and prosper in every area of life.

'HE SHALL BE LIKE A TREE PLANTED BY THE RIVERS OF WATER, THAT BRINGS FORTH ITS FRUIT IN ITS SEASON'

[PSALM 1:3]

Nature study experiments at school have had many of us planting seeds in dusty soil or even moistened cotton wool. The object of the lesson was to *look* for signs of growth. Those seeds may have begun well but most would end up as degenerate, alien plants.

There are three specific tell-tale signs that reveal whether or not someone is truly flourishing or not.

One of the first signs of health is *appearance*. A flourishing plant is attractive and pleasant to look at because of its lovely fresh foliage. Likewise, the countenance of those who are flourishing will be radiant and shine with His joy. Everyone likes to be around such people, and even in the midst of challenges such people maintain their joy.

You will also recognise those who are flourishing by their *behaviour*. As deciduous and evergreen trees are identified by their behaviour patterns, so believers are identifiable by their behaviour patterns. Some come to church but never enter into worship or participate in the service. Others adopt a cynical or negative attitude about anything and everything. On the other hand, those who are flourishing will lean towards life and worship God with a sense of wholeheartedness. The words on their lips will be positive and uplifting.

Finally, you can identify a flourishing life by its *fruit*. The first instruction God gave humanity was to be fruitful and multiply. If you are bearing fruit, you should be seeing increase and expansion across the spectrum of your life – clear evidence that God is working in your life.

Of course we all need to be mindful of seasons and that time is required to see things come to maturity, but living by God's ways promises that the harvest is guaranteed in our lives.

'THE RIGHTEOUS SHALL
FLOURISH LIKE A
PALM TREE,
HE SHALL GROW LIKE A
CEDAR IN LEBANON'

[PSALM 92:12]

The Bible often uses the analogy of trees and plants to illustrate the spiritual condition of our lives. For example, Psalm 92 says:

'The righteous shall flourish like a palm tree, he shall grow like a cedar in Lebanon.' [Psalm 92:12]

The cedars of Lebanon were considered to be among the greatest of all trees in the ancient world and are frequently mentioned in the scriptures. Once plentiful, they are now somewhat rare, but the attributes of this kind of tree are what God intends for our lives.

Tall and beautiful, the cedars of Lebanon symbolise strength and magnificence. The fact that they were such colossal trees, growing to over 100 feet, meant they required a lot of nourishment, but their purpose went beyond mere visual splendour. The Bible says:

'The trees of the Lord are full of sap, the cedars of Lebanon which He planted, where the birds make their nests.' [Psalm 104:16,17]

The cedars of Lebanon 'which He planted' weren't only impressive to look at but they served a greater purpose. They produced exceptionally good wood that was both aromatic and durable. So superior was the wood that Solomon imported it for the temple in Jerusalem and other building projects.

This analogy also relates to us. Such people stand tall and strong above the rest; they are firmly established, resilient and thriving in every area of life. Such Kingdom-minded people understand they have a purpose far greater than themselves and are committed to resource the work of God upon the earth by providing from their substance.

This is a great illustration of a blessed and flourishing life, planted and nourished by God Himself – a picture of what you are actually destined to look like.

'YOU WILL KNOW
THEM BY THEIR
FRUITS'

[MATTHEW 7:16]

The very first instruction God gave humanity was simply this, *'Be fruitful and multiply.'* [Genesis 1:28]

It isn't actually an *option* for believers to be fruitful, it is a *responsibility* that carries consequence. In Mark 11 we read a sobering story. Jesus was hungry so He went over to a fig tree to see if He could find any fruit. All it offered was green leaves, so He cursed it. Obviously we are courting danger by putting on the same facade. The reason for our existence is to build the Kingdom and impact the lives of others.

A person's belief is revealed by their actions, and a church's belief is revealed by what it does. Jesus said:

'And these signs will follow those who believe...' [Mark 16:17]

The fruit of your life doesn't lie. Throughout the Bible, we read of the blessings (or signs) that follow those who live according to God's principles. For instance, success and prosperity are the promise of God in Joshua 1:8. If you keep living by His principles, no matter what comes against you, you are a candidate for success and prosperity.

By appearances, the Pharisees were the most respected religious scholars of the time, but Jesus pointed out the futility of their works because they never produced any fruit that benefitted others. He said:

'You will know them by their fruits. Do men gather grapes from thornbushes or figs from thistles? Even so, every good tree bears good fruit, but a bad tree bears bad fruit.' [Matthew 7:16,17]

Whether we like it or not, people will judge us by the fruit of our lives. Sometimes their particular mindset may colour their perception, but do others look at you and see good fruit? A flourishing church creates an environment where good people produce good fruit. I hope you live in such an environment!

'UNLESS THE LORD
BUILDS THE HOUSE,
THEY LABOUR IN VAIN
WHO BUILD IT'

[PSALM 127:1]

How can any of us know that what we are sowing our lives into will prove fruitful and productive on the scale of eternity? Ask yourself the following questions.

What am I building?

Jesus said He would build His Church, and I believe there is nothing greater we can do than commit to help build what He said He would build.

> *'On this rock I will build My church, and the gates of Hades shall not prevail against it.'* [Matthew 16:18]

Sadly, there are those who continually criticise the Church, not realising that instead of building it, they are tearing down something very precious to God. In this life, we have the opportunity to build so many things – from a marriage and family, to a home and a career, to the testimony or legacy that we will leave behind us. Some people build the wrong things into their lives – they build walls instead of unity in their relationships, or they build a mountain of debt instead of a mountain of resource in their finances. Instead of building a testimony to a life flourishing in God, they are left with a sense of failure and futility.

If you want to flourish in life, everything you build should line up with or complement what He is building – His Church.

What do I love?

Jesus loved His Church and gave Himself for her. If you want to know what someone really loves, watch what they give themselves to. For example, avid gardeners spend their time gardening; musicians give their time to listening to or playing music. Radical followers of Jesus Christ involve themselves in their Father's labour. As Jesus said:

> *'For where your treasure is, there your heart will be also.'*
>
> [Matthew 6:21]

If you want to flourish in life, love what He loves and give yourself to it.

What am I adding to?

What are you contributing to on a daily basis? Some add nothing more than humanistic opinions, quarrelsome arguments, or rumours and strife. All they are adding is confusion and chaos, where nothing good can flourish.

> *'And the Lord **added** to the church daily those who were being saved.'*
> [Acts 2:47]

A flourishing life will add to or enhance the work of the Lord. There are numerous things you can contribute towards building God's Kingdom, such as a positive attitude, godly thinking, words of life and an unwavering commitment to the House of God.

The great and wonderful thing is that as we add to His purposes, God also adds to our lives. Jesus promised:

> *'But seek first the Kingdom of God and His righteousness, and all these things shall be **added** to you.'* [Matthew 6:33]

What am I confronting?

Here is a thought that many believers prefer to avoid. Jesus was never one to stand back and complacently or helplessly shrug off immature behaviour. He always confronted poor thinking, particularly among the religious leaders of the day.

> *'Then Jesus went into the temple of God and drove out all those who bought and sold in the temple, and overturned the tables of the moneychangers and the seats of those who sold doves.'*
> [Matthew 21:12-13]

In confronting the attitudes of the merchants, Jesus turned things right side up – the way they should be. There are many attitudes and mindsets that need to be confronted and turned right side up in order for the Church to thrive. If you want to flourish, you will need to confront your attitudes and align your thinking to God's purpose for His Church.

'THAT YOU, ALWAYS HAVING ALL SUFFICIENCY IN ALL THINGS, HAVE AN ABUNDANCE FOR EVERY GOOD WORK'

[2 CORINTHIANS 9:8]

What am I supplying?

God's plan is for His Church to be a place of provision, or, as the Old Testament refers to it, a *storehouse*. It is a place where people can come and receive from the abundance of the supply.

The House of God, besides providing a place where you can worship God and receive the Word, should also be able to provide people with other things, such as pastoral care, crisis intervention, prayer and meaningful fellowship. When people have needs, we (the Church) should be in a position to meet them. Imagine if someone came to the Church for help and we had to turn them away because we had nothing to give them? When people are floundering in life, the Church is where they should find the practical and spiritual sustenance that helps to encourage and restore them. Paul describes God's plan of supply:

'And God is able to make all grace abound toward you, that you, always having all **sufficiency** *in all things, have an* **abundance** *for every good work.'* [2 Corinthians 9:8]

There are two key concepts relating to supply and provision in this portion of scripture.

Sufficiency relates to you and your needs. God's plan is that you always have *'all* sufficiency in *all* things'. Sufficient doesn't mean only enough to get by on – it means *all* you need. Paul wrote:

'And my God shall supply all your need according to His riches in glory by Christ Jesus.' [Philippians 4:19]

Abundance relates to your increased capacity to supply and provide for the needs of others. God has gone further than ensuring that only your needs are met, but that *'you have an abundance for every good work.'* His blessing of abundance is not for you to store up for yourself, but His purpose is to resource you to be an agent of supply.

'BELOVED, I PRAY THAT YOU MAY PROSPER IN ALL THINGS AND BE IN HEALTH, JUST AS YOUR SOUL PROSPERS'

[3 JOHN 2]

I honestly love seeing people prosper and increase in life, and I could fill a book with stories of people who have planted themselves in our church and are realising their dreams.

A great example is our worship pastor, Darlene Zschech, who has earned world-wide influence and respect in the area of praise and worship. Many see the fruit of her life today but aren't fully aware of the passion and devotion with which Darlene and her husband Mark have planted themselves in God's House. For many years they have whole-heartedly sown their lives into building the Kingdom and faithfully carved out a path that has inspired many others. It is no wonder that they are flourishing.

There are many pastors who would love to have Darlene as their worship leader, but could they handle a worship pastor more famous than them? If I was insecure or threatened by the success of any of my team, I would more than likely suppress them. However, I know that I need to build a church that is big enough to fulfil their dreams.

In 3 John 2, it describes how prosperity and health are the results of a prosperous soul. Those who are planted in the House and share the load constitute the healthy soul of a church. Their commitment and contribution causes the local House and greater Body of Christ to prosper and flourish.

Paul revealed four distinct attitudes or levels of involvement among Christians in his letter to Timothy:

*'Command those who are rich in this present age not to be haughty, nor to trust in uncertain riches but in the living God, who gives us richly all things to **enjoy**. Let them do good, that they be rich in **good works**, ready to **give**, willing to **share**, storing up for themselves a good foundation for the time to come, that they may lay hold on eternal life.'* [1 Timothy 6:17-19]

In the following pages, allow me to examine four levels of Christian growth and maturity and how they contribute to and build the Church.

'[TRUST] IN THE LIVING GOD, WHO GIVES US RICHLY ALL THINGS TO ENJOY'

[1 TIMOTHY 6:17]

FIRST LEVEL: ENJOYMENT

The first level of Christianity is enjoyment. Paul wrote:
'[Trust] in the living God, who gives us richly all things to enjoy.'

[1 Timothy 6:17]

God has given us so many things to enjoy. Paul warns against trusting in uncertain riches, but the issue is not so much about riches as it is one of trust. God doesn't have a problem with us having things – He has a problem with *things having us*!

There is nothing wrong with Christians enjoying life and having a good sense of humour. Sadly, some believers are far too serious about everything. I've always believed that Christians should be the most magnetic people – the ones everyone wants to hang out with because they are so much fun – the life and soul of any party. I love, for example, the enthusiasm and excitement of new Christians. They are like sponges, eagerly soaking up everything that their new life in Christ has to offer.

The focus of this *first level of Christian growth* is about you and the exciting discovery of what God has in store for *your* life. For instance, teachings on blessing or success will be about *your* gain; worship will be about *your* personal preference of songs; and friendships will be built around the good times *you* are having.

There are many things God intends for us to enjoy, but enjoyment is not *all* that He has for those who are planted in His House.

It is far better to enjoy church than to endure it, but if our Christianity only extends to enjoyment, we only scratch the surface of God's purposes. There is so much more.

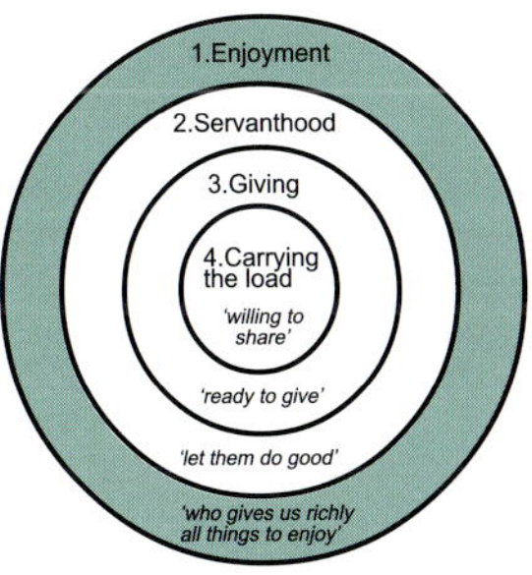

Those who are

planted in the

House of the Lord

shall flourish in

the courts of our

God. They shall

still bear fruit

in old age: They

shall be fresh

and flourishing.

'LET THEM DO GOOD,
THAT THEY BE RICH
IN GOOD WORKS'

[1 TIMOTHY 6:18]

SECOND LEVEL: SERVANTHOOD

Τhe second level of involvement in church life is servanthood. *'Let them do good, that they be rich in good works.'* [1 Timothy 6:18]

Christians who rise to this second level are those who have added to their enjoyment by committing to serve in God's House. Volunteers such as ushers or helpers who serve others with a willing heart, make a valuable contribution to building the Church on the earth.

Every year our Hillsong Conference draws thousands of delegates from all over the world. The conference always has a great line-up of internationally-recognised speakers and musicians, but we have discovered that the greatest praise on the delegate feedback forms is always reserved for the spirit of the volunteers.

Our contingent of volunteers at Hillsong Conference is now well over two thousand. They are the ones who arrive before anyone else in the morning (to set up) and leave well after everyone else in the evenings (after cleaning up). They not only do it selflessly, but they do it cheerfully. As the Bible instructs us:

'Serve the Lord with gladness.' [Psalm 100:2]

Some Christians serve in God's House, but they do it grudgingly or out of obligation. Somewhere along the line, they lost their enjoyment. While serving is part of 'doing good,' the challenge is to serve with a spirit of gladness.

The key is to still keep enjoying God's House (first level), and apply yourself to serve Him with good works (second level). What is the point of giving your time and not enjoying it?

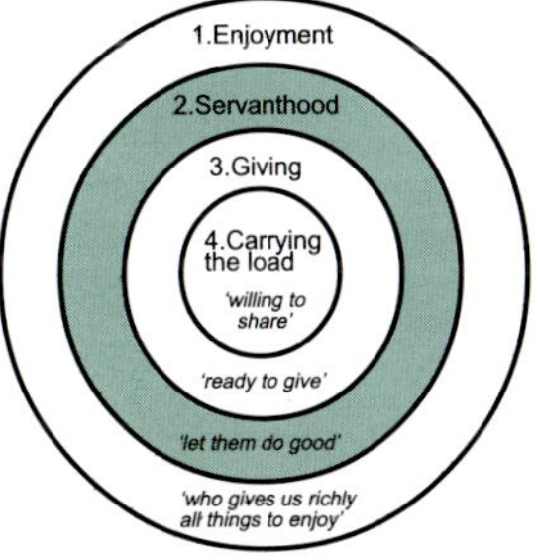

'...READY TO GIVE...'

[1 TIMOTHY 6:18]

THIRD LEVEL: GIVING

The third level of Christianity is a revelation of giving. The verse continues ... *'ready to give.'* [1 Timothy 6:18]

It is wonderful to watch new Christians rise from the level of enjoyment to become actively involved in serving in God's House, and then go on to gain a revelation of what the spirit of giving is all about.

Some people are happy to volunteer or serve, but are much less enthusiastic when challenged to give. They can end up limiting their own lives because they never discover that it really is *more blessed to give than to receive.*

Whenever a teacher addresses the subject of giving or finance, such people are immediately resistant or defensive. The reality is that people will always rise to defend the thing they love, and sadly, 'the love of money' is an attitude that prevents many from advancing in the purposes of God.

If you want to move to a deeper level of involvement in God's House, you will need to expand in the area of giving. Test yourself. When it is time to receive the tithes and offerings in church, what is your response? Do you come prepared with your tithe and are you excited about giving, or do you react in defence or annoyance?

To move to the third level of Christianity requires a spirit of liberality and a revelation of the words of Jesus:

'Freely you have received, freely give.' [Matthew 10:8]

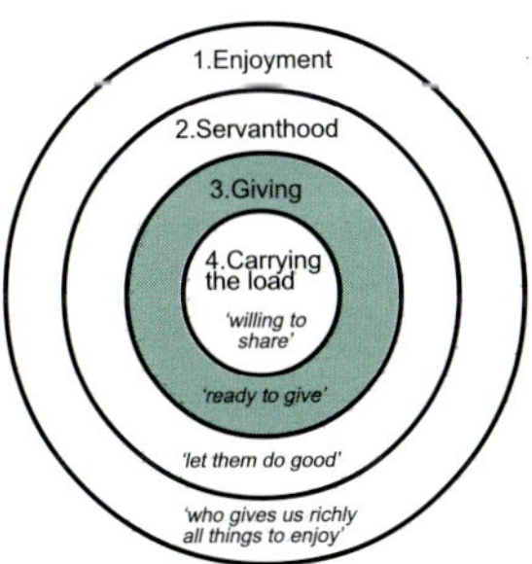

'...WILLING TO
SHARE'

[1 TIMOTHY 6:18]

FOURTH LEVEL: SHARING THE LOAD

If a malnourished orphan was led on to the platform of a church, most of those observing would be willing to give generously for the provision of the child. But how many would be prepared to take the child home?

The fourth level of Christianity is about carrying the load, or as Paul put it, *'willing to share.'* [1 Timothy 6:18]

Christians who share the load are the ones who will do whatever it takes to fulfil the vision. Religion has developed a concept that clergy is separate from laity, but there is nothing biblical about that belief. A flourishing church involves more people than the senior leadership alone. Paul described the purpose of the five-fold ministry:

'For the equipping of the saints for the work of the ministry, for the edifying of the body of Christ.' [Ephesians 4:12]

Apostles, prophets, evangelists, pastors and teachers are given to inspire and teach everyone involved. The 'work of the ministry' is actually the responsibility of every believer.

Church life is comprised of all four types of believers and at the core of a healthy church are those who *own the vision* and help *carry the load* of responsibility.

There have been many in our congregation who have sacrificed for many years to finance our new building and today, many new believers are enjoying the benefits of those who were ready to give and willing to share.

Plant yourself in God's House and you will begin to flourish, and as you do, you will keep expanding and moving into new levels of responsibility and growth.

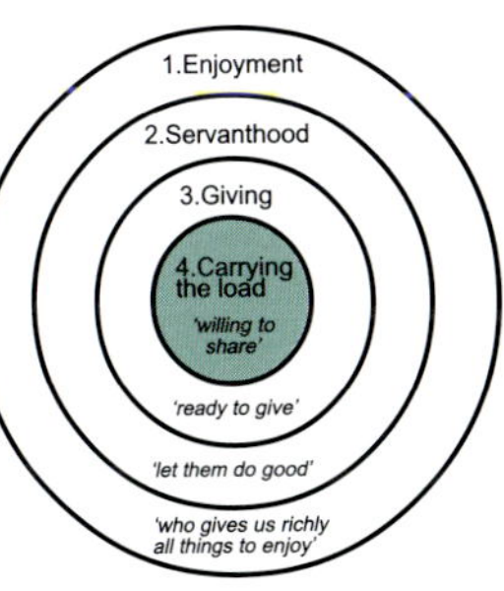

'I WILL BLESS YOU
AND MAKE YOUR
NAME GREAT;
AND YOU SHALL BE A
BLESSING.'

[GENESIS 12:2]

Mother Theresa spent her life attending to poverty-stricken people and gathered phenomenal resource to relieve them from that poverty.

People mistakenly believe that Jesus taught against money, but the real issue is that Jesus taught about our **attitude** *towards money*. The problem isn't money, but our thinking towards it. If there is one subject people really get uptight about, it is the subject of money.

Over the centuries, there has been a lot of upside-down thinking about wealth and finance that has limited the effectiveness of the Church. For too long God's people have been discouraged from flourishing financially and the result has been that they have been limited in their ability to make a huge impact in blessing others.

In Psalm 92, the analogy of the flourishing tree that bears fruit in its season reveals the purpose of God. If fruit remains on the tree, it never blesses or provides for anyone. We are called to be fruitful and multiply in order to fulfil God's purpose on the earth to be a blessing to others.

God's purpose for blessing us is revealed in these words:

'I will make you a great nation, I will bless you and make your name great; and you shall be a blessing.' [Genesis 12:2]

The purpose of God's promise to Abraham is clear '... *and you shall be a blessing*!' The blessing and influence didn't stop with Abraham and his own well-being – it was about being a blessing to others.

Why does God want you to flourish and prosper in life? So you can live well beyond yourself and bless others.

'FOR AS A MAN
THINKS,
SO IS HE'

[PROVERBS 23:7]

Those who are
planted in the
House of the Lord
shall flourish in
the courts of our
God. They shall
still bear fruit
in old age; They
shall be fresh
and flourishing.

What you allow to flourish in your thinking has a powerful impact on who you are and what you become. The New King James version of the Bible puts it like this:

'For as he [a man] thinks in his heart, so is he.' [Proverbs 23:7]

When you allow your heart and thinking to line up with the Word of God, you will begin to become the person He says you are. Sadly, there are Christians who once thrived in the purposes of God, but have now become stunted and stale – all because they indulged in thoughts that should have been weeded out immediately.

Thoughts which are negative, cynical or defeatist are all contrary to the heart of God. So are feelings of bitterness and rejection. Jesus warned us that offences will come, but the danger is in allowing an offence to dominate your thoughts.

The Apostle Paul warns us to be diligent:

'... lest any root of bitterness springing up cause trouble, and by this many become defiled.' [Hebrews 12:15]

Allow an offence to take root and you may find yourself dealing with a *stronghold* of bitterness. Paul tells us how to effectively deal with such thoughts:

'... pulling down strongholds, casting down arguments and every high thing that exalts itself against the knowledge of God, bringing every thought into captivity to the obedience of Christ.'

[2 Corinthians 10:4,5]

Quickly take negative thoughts, wrong perceptions or offences captive before they take root. Arrest them before they sabotage your life. The progression towards a stronghold always starts with a thought, so it is vital to keep your thinking clean, clear and lined up with God's Word.

'BRINGING EVERY
THOUGHT INTO
CAPTIVITY TO THE
OBEDIENCE OF CHRIST'

[2 CORINTHIANS 10:5]

One thought, unchallenged, can tragically change the course of your life. The progression from the seed of a thought to a flourishing stronghold has four specific stages, according to 2 Corinthians 10:4-5.

1. Thoughts

'Bringing every thought into captivity to the obedience of Christ.'
Paul urges us to take every thought captive and line it up with the Word because, if left to roam free, it can become a potential threat to God's purposes. It is easier to pull a weed out of a garden when it is still small so arrest your thoughts in the early stages before they take deep root and become a 'high thing.'

2. High things

'Every high thing that exalts itself against the knowledge of God.'
When a thought becomes a 'high thing', it begins to dominate or constantly preoccupy your mind. At night, your mind may race with thoughts or fears that all seem so much bigger than they really are. It is these preoccupying thoughts that cause you to lose perspective as 'high things' elevate themselves above God's Word.

3. Arguments

'Casting down arguments.'
Once a thought has become a high thing, it can progress to an argument. No longer is it only in your mind but you could make an argument out of it. Defending such thinking shows that it has started to make sense to you and your perspective has begun to blur.

4. Strongholds

'Pulling down strongholds.'
A stronghold is exactly what it implies: something that has taken a strong hold of you. At this stage, it isn't so easy to weed it out. When wrong thoughts become strongholds in your life, they will choke your potential to flourish.

'BLESSED IS THE
MAN WHO ENDURES
TEMPTATION'

[JAMES 1:12]

The lure and trap of pornography, particularly on the Internet, is a perfect example of the progression we have been talking about. A 'seed thought' is entertained and allowed to develop into a 'stronghold' in the mind.

An individual falling into this trap begins by indulging a *thought*. Before long, they are *preoccupied* in their thought processes. Soon they are *arguing* that what they are involved in is acceptable and won't harm anyone. However, the tragedy of this behaviour is a 'not-easily-broken' *stronghold* that has been the demise of many individuals, marriages and families.

Temptation succeeds when someone is drawn away and enticed by their own desires, rather than God's purposes. What is 'more pleasant to their soul' overshadows what is right in the sight of their God. James used the analogy of conception and birth, except that instead of Life being established, death results – death to the purposes of God in your life. As James wrote:

> *'But each one is tempted when he is drawn away by his own desires and enticed. Then, when desire has conceived, it gives birth to sin; and sin, when it is full-grown, brings forth death.'* [James 1:14,15]

Entertain an alluring thought for long enough and it won't stay a thought for long. If not dealt with immediately, it can become a fully-fledged lifestyle that is contrary to God's plans for a flourishing life.

Such deceptive illusions never show the whole picture or ramifications. The husband who is tempted to embark on an adulterous affair isn't focusing on the hurt and devastation, the financial loss, or feelings of shame and guilt that will come to his family.

Resisting temptation the moment you see it is essential, because it can quickly develop into a thriving issue or stronghold. Don't make the mistake of toying with it, because it *will* jeopardise your future.

'THEN HE SPOKE A
PARABLE TO THEM,
THAT MEN ALWAYS
OUGHT TO PRAY AND
NOT LOSE HEART'

[LUKE 18:1]

It is a presumptuous person who thinks they can live without prayer. Some people call themselves Christians but they never take the time to communicate with God. As a result, their relationship with Him fails to flourish in the way that it could or should.

God created us to know and enjoy the blessing of a personal relationship with Him. In the Garden of Eden, Adam walked and talked with God without inhibition, and it was only when sin separated him from God that he hid himself. Many people still hide from God today, not realising that through Jesus Christ they can be perfectly reconciled. This is what the Bible says:

'Then He spoke a parable to them, that men always ought to pray and not lose heart.' [Luke 18:1]

Sadly, there are many who find prayer difficult and the reason why they lose heart is because wrong perceptions or traditions about prayer keep them starved of a personal relationship with God.

Jesus was in constant communication with the Father and never acted without His instruction. We can also read how Jesus communicated with those who were close to Him. He didn't only teach His disciples spiritual truths, but He also talked naturally with them. They were able to be honest and open, and ask Him anything.

This is a wonderful pattern of what our relationship with God can be like. Your communication with Him need not be based on repetitious, religious prayers but instead you can enjoy a close, intimate relationship with Him. I enjoy taking time out to speak with the Lord while out running, driving my car or even sitting on an aeroplane. When your prayer life flourishes, you feel its effect across every area of your life.

'BUT HE WHO
ENDURES TO THE END
WILL BE SAVED'

[MATTHEW 10:22]

When you begin to flourish in life, others will certainly notice – but not everyone will be happy about it. The blessing of God will draw the attention of others, but it will also attract its share of opposition. So what can you do in the midst of persecution?

Commit to greater blessing

'For when tribulation or persecution arises because of the word, immediately he stumbles.' [Matthew 13:21]

Our natural instinct would be to draw back, but be determined to stand your ground and refuse to lower your stand. In fact, why not commit to flourish even more in the face of persecution!

Whistle a different tune

'But I say to you … pray for those who spitefully use you and persecute you.' [Matthew 5:44]

Instead of reacting according to the ways of the world, respond according to the way of the Word. Don't let those who persecute you rule your spirit but rather become an agent of blessing. It will keep your spirit free.

Keep your course

'And you will be hated by all for My name's sake. But he who endures to the end will be saved.' [Matthew 10:22]

No matter what you are facing, stay on course because God is faithful to His promises.

In the midst of persecution, refuse to draw back or allow others to rule your spirit. Having done all, stand and keep your course.

The seeds of the highest quality that God has placed in you are destined to flourish and prosper. Don't settle for anything less. Let your life bear testimony to what you believe in and let others see those signs following.

'[THEY] WERE FRUITFUL
AND INCREASED
ABUNDANTLY,
MULTIPLIED AND GREW
EXCEEDINGLY MIGHTY'

[EXODUS 1:7]

Human nature, when left to its own devices, is prone to settling down and becoming comfortable. The biggest enemy to a flourishing life is complacency, which is why every believer and every church needs a commitment to maintain and empower the momentum.

The fact is that healthy things grow, so one of my highest priorities is to keep our church healthy. It is complacency that makes Christianity and church life dull and mediocre, but it is momentum that keeps people moving forward to the next level.

As Senior Pastor of a growing church, here are five things that I believe you can do to help your church flourish.

Your testimony

The Apostle Paul describes believers as 'living epistles' who are 'known and read by all men.' When your life is flourishing in God, others will be inspired by your testimony and example.

Your attention

There is nothing more rewarding than preaching to a receptive congregation. Don't allow yourself to go through the motions at church, but always be hungry for the Word of God.

Your presence

Would you be missed if you didn't make it to church? The reality is that those who are growing in God not only attend church, they presence themselves there and contribute to the atmosphere.

Your gifts and talents

God uses the different strengths and talents of individuals to add to the church. You have unique gifts that can build your local church.

Your health

Every church needs a core of people who are spiritually healthy. Their words and example bring life and energy to the church. Believe for God to bless you with a healthy spirit, mind and body so you are unhindered in serving Him.

The decisions you make will position you to flourish or flounder in life. Ask yourself the following questions and determine whether you are positioned to thrive.

Are you planted?

'*For he shall be like a tree planted by the waters...*' [Jeremiah 17:8]

If you are not planted anywhere, you will not grow. Likewise, if you are planted in the wrong environment, you will not produce the best fruit. A tree planted by the waters is in a good position to receive regular nourishment.

Every believer needs to be planted in a local church where they can thrive in their gifts and talents, and where there is plenty of encouragement and room for growth. If you are planted in a place where you are limited and contained, you are unlikely to see the seed of the highest quality within you reach its full potential.

How easily can you be uprooted?

'*...which spreads out its roots by the river.*' [Jeremiah 17:8]

When the roots of a tree are widely spread and run deep into the earth, it is not easy to uproot or move them. It is the same with those who are planted in God's House and are actively involved in the spectrum of church life. They are the ones who are always there, participating in cell groups, helping with the children and youth, and financially committed to church projects. Because their friendships and relationships are built around the church family, it would be a great upheaval if they had to uproot themselves and move away.

Compare these to those who stay on the fringe of church life and never allow themselves to become completely involved or committed to anything. It is easy for them to uproot themselves and drift away, preventing themselves from flourishing the way God intended.

Those who are

planted in the

House of the Lord

shall flourish in

the courts of our

God. They shall

still bear fruit

in old age: They

shall be fresh

and flourishing.

'... AND WILL NOT FEAR
WHEN HEAT COMES;
BUT HER LEAF WILL
BE GREEN ...'

[JEREMIAH 17:8]

Can you take the heat?

'*And will not fear when heat comes.*' [Jeremiah 17:8]

The Word doesn't say '*if* heat comes' but '*when* heat comes.' The Bible never promises us a life without tests or challenges, and there will always be obstacles to overcome. Let me assure you – the heat will come.

A flourishing life is not thrown off course by obstacles or a bit of heat. Don't be like those who draw back when opposition comes their way – stand firm. The psalmist wrote:

'*We went through fire and through water; but You brought us out to rich fulfillment.*' [Psalm 66:12]

If you are planted in the House of the Lord, no matter what happens, you can weather the storm. There will be times when you will go through the fire, but you will emerge strong and victorious.

Is your spiritual health a priority?

'*But her leaf will be green.*' [Jeremiah 17:8]

Lush, green foliage is the evidence of a healthy plant, but that doesn't mean you stop watering it. You must commit to maintaining the health of your spiritual life.

The reality is that the older we get, the harder it is to keep our level of physical health and fitness. The same applies to our spiritual lives. Mature Christians can think they know it all and that they don't have to apply themselves as much as they used to in their spiritual growth.

Never take your spiritual life for granted, because you will lose your strength and become weak. Don't neglect to feed your spirit daily. Today there is so much resource available to build up your spirit and your local church should be the place where you are constantly receiving spiritual nourishment.

'...AND WILL NOT
BE ANXIOUS IN THE YEAR
OF DROUGHT,
NOR WILL CEASE FROM
YIELDING FRUIT'

[JEREMIAH 17:8]

Are you ruled by the seasons?

'*[They] will not be anxious in the year of drought.*' [Jeremiah 17:8]
Some people never move forward in life because they are ruled by the seasons. Many are ruled by the economic climate – whenever the dollar takes a dive, they become fearful about the future. Because their future hinges on these possibilities, they never invest any time or energy into building anything substantial.

Those who are planted in God's House are not afraid of dry seasons because they understand that seasons have an end. They are the ones who continue putting God first when their finances are tight or circumstances are rocky. Paul wrote:

'*And let us not grow weary while doing good, for in due **season** we shall reap if we do not lose heart.*' [Galatians 6:9]

Is fruitfulness a lifestyle?

'*Nor will cease from yielding fruit.*' [Jeremiah 17:8]
Psalm 92 promises that those who are planted in the House of the Lord 'shall still bear fruit in old age.' There are those who only give to others when their circumstances are favourable, but for those who are planted in God's House, giving is a lifestyle. They give generously from the fruit of their lives, whether they are in or out of season.

The fact is that fruit that remains on a tree doesn't benefit anyone. Sadly, there are those who are fruitful but never surrender their fruit to bless others. Remember, God's will for His people to flourish and prosper goes further than our own lives.

You have every opportunity to flourish in the House of God if you choose to be planted and to allow your roots to go down deep. Be prepared to take the heat and to be consistent in the seasons. Always give your spiritual health priority, and build a lifestyle that is constantly blessing others with the fruit of your life.

'Those who are planted in the House of the Lord shall flourish in the courts of our God' [Hillsong Church 2003]

When Bobbie and I moved to Australia in 1978, we had only been married a year. One could possibly see the seeds of potential within us, but we didn't have much fruit.

Nevertheless, we began sowing our lives into the work of the ministry because we had a vision and a dream to build a flourishing church. When we held our initial services in the Baulkham Hills School Hall, we began with a congregation of 45 people. At that time, we could never have imagined that over twenty years later, we would be pastoring what is possibly Australia's largest church.

Over the years, we began to be fruitful and multiply, and thousands have come to know Christ through our weekend services. When I look across our congregation each week, it blesses me to see the many people who decided to plant themselves in God's House and have gone from strength to strength. The result is that they are 'fresh and flourishing' and the fruit of their lives is evident to all.

Who could have foreseen the number of lives that have been impacted by Hillsong Church? Such an abundance of fruit and increase is only known to God.

The fact is that *you can count how many seeds there are in an orange, but you cannot count how many oranges there are in a seed.*

God has deposited seeds of the highest quality within you that have the potential to build a flourishing life beyond your greatest dreams. My prayer is that you will plant yourself in a local church where you will be nourished and bring forth all that is within you.